My First Year as an Internet Entrepreneur

My First Year as an Internet Entrepreneur

*"In the end,
your success will speak for itself."*

Patrick Bet-David

●●●●●●●●●●●●●●●●●●●●●●●●●●●●●●●●●●●●●●●

My First Year as an Internet Entrepreneur

●●●●●●●●●●●●●●●●●●●●●●●●●●●●●●●●●●●●●●●

From Financial Insecurity to Financial Stability

Roberto Zanon

My First Year as an Internet Entrepreneur

From Financial Insecurity to Financial Stability

ISBN 978-1523760312 paperback

Table of Contents

Hello, My Name Is...

Hello, before we start with this book, I would like to tell you a few things about me that will help us connect better.

I promise, it won't be long, and I'll try to make it as interesting as possible (I know quite a few marketing tricks you know).

My name is Roberto Zanon, I was born in 1981, in Athens, Greece. I still live there and I have a younger sister and my mother. My dad was killed in a bike accident when I was 18 years old.

By the time of this writing I am not a millionaire (yet), but I am able to support a nice lifestyle doing the things I like, from wherever I like.

It would be a lie to tell you that I have already achieved financial independence, but, at least, I can work from the comfort of my home and cover my expenses without having to deal with a lousy boss day in and day out.

I am not living the big life which I intend to, but I am quite happy with my lifestyle up to now. I try to improve myself day by day, little by little. I train every day, I eat healthily, I work many hours each day and I study a lot in a variety of topics like anthropology, human nature, psychology, marketing, sales, economics etc.

My end-game plan is to be as healthy and happy as possible every day and financially free before I get 40.

A general overview

During my school years, I was not the most popular kid in my class. I wasn't a nerd either. Just an introvert, an **average guy who** was not that popular. I had a few friends I was hanging around with, and I had minimal interaction with girls (don't ask me why).
The same pattern held true for the rest of my high-school and post-graduate studies.

Although I considered myself to be a smart guy, my social performance was inadequate at best.

For the biggest part of my life, I sucked in every pillar of life (a big time).

I was chubby, with very few friends (and even fewer girlfriends) and don't even get me started on my orientation about wealth.

After finishing my master's degree in the UK (on wireless systems), I came back to Greece to find my first job. And so I did.

Although not much of a job (I was a presales engineer), it gave me a pretty accurate understanding of what a corporate environment is and helped me pay my bills.

Having no other influences at that time, I considered this a "normal" way of doing things.

After a couple of years, this first company went bankrupted and I had to find a new job. Although I found a new job quickly, something inside me was telling me that something wasn't right.

I remained for a few months in this company and after my contract was over, I decided to leave for somewhere else.

Same position different company. I didn't like that either. That was the point where I hit my highest anti-social moment in my life. I had absolutely zero interest for the job or the people around me.

Although I was "politically correct" with my duties, I wasn't talking to almost anyone, and when I was, I tried to keep that to a minimum level. I was performing just the bare minimum when it came to the job and way below that when it came to socializing with my colleagues.
I didn't like them, and they didn't like me. I guess this is not the way things work in

companies, so after a few months, they fired me, making a big favor to both of us.

My last day job ever was on a call center as a call agent. I was making cold calls to potential customers selling telephone subscriptions.

Intelligence and knowledge wise I was way overqualified and that was obvious right away. After a few weeks I was given the department manager position and they promised they would give me another promotion very soon.

Once again, something inside me didn't feel quite right. My subconscious did know better I guess. Not sure how to explain this innate repulsion about my day job. I didn't really know where it came from, but I did know it was 100% real.

So after a few months, I quit this job as well, starting my first company.

Milestone 1: let's get fit

Almost in parallel, I realized that if I ever wanted to have any success with girls I had to lose these extra pounds and become more athletic.

And boy did I deliver. I lost about 30 pounds and I gained some nice sexual experiences along the way.

Losing those pounds, changed me in two fundamental ways.

First and foremost, I felt capable of doing something for the first time in my life. It might not be that clear to some of you, but losing weight (while your body tends to gain weight very easily) isn't an easy task. I was raised as a chubby kid and so my body "liked" that state - it still does actually, but I say "no" to it very often.

I was 100% in control of my emotions as long as my eating was concerned. I was on a very strict diet and was spending many hours in the gym for six days a week.

That was my first a-h-a moment. I realized that nothing is impossible if you set your mind on it. I learned to be self-disciplined, which I still consider it to be one of the most important skills when it comes to success.

Health was now a vital part of my life, and although I had no success on the wealth front, I started very slowly to gain some momentum.

Milestone 2: average people cry (a lot)

No matter how cheesy this might sound, my second milestone was a girl. Or rather, the break up with her.

Having improved my **image (reproduction value)** considerably, I was having a greater success with girls. I was getting laid with more and better girls and I liked it.

And then I met her. She was smoking hot, young, funny and full of energy. I was dying for her and she liked me as well. Although I have to admit it, she didn't like me as much as I did.

My relationship with her was like a dream. At that time, I was thinking she was perfect and I wouldn't want her to change a thing.

Being only an **average person** myself (only with a six-pack), eventually she dumped me, dropping me dead.

I was devastated for over six months, and I can actually say that this period was by far the worst of my life, from a psychological point of view.

Making the usual retrospection, I now laugh with my reaction and I keep thinking what an idiot I was. But at the time, she meant the world to me, and losing her was absolutely the worst thing that could happen to me.

Today, if I had the chance to tell her something, I would thank her for doing so. It might be hurtful but she taught me the hard way, that in life, **you have to be someone of value** to gain things.

Nobody is going to offer you stuff for free. You either deserve it or not. And I was clearly not "deserving" her at that point.

Of course this realization, took place quite a few years later and only after I had found my "source of enlightenment" - at least up to now.

Milestone 3: enlightenment

Someday, a few years later, a very good friend of mine found a forum about *game* in my city. We thought it was quite interesting and decided to give it a go. It turned out it was a quite helpful community of people who had self-improvement as their main goal. What began as a *game*, it turned out to be a race to self-improvement and development.

Very fast, I became obsessed with the whole idea of becoming a better man. I became obsessed to improve every aspect of my life I could.

This might sound simple, but trust me it is not. For someone like me that I had been swallowing the blue pill of social conditioning for many many years, hearing all these new ideas wasn't easy to accept.

I was now taught that almost everything I was doing up till then was "wrong". Health, wealth and relationships wise.

I was told that every positive outcome I had up to this point was by chance, and if I wanted to improve my results in all sectors, I had to do something about it.

If I wanted to be in a good condition and healthy **praying to God wasn't enough.** I had to understand how the human body works, and what is beneficial for my health. I had to learn what to eat, how to exercise properly, how to sleep well, and how to reduce my stress levels.

If I wanted to have more success with both men and women, I had to understand how humans "work" from an evolutionary point of view and then implement all this knowledge in order to improve my social interactions with them.

If I ever wanted to make lots of money, formal education and linear way of thinking wouldn't cut it. I had to study how successful people have done it. I had to work not only harder but in a smarter way as well.

Luckily, my mentor, Iraklis Kiriakakis, has a very powerful style to captivate your interest. He made every story, narration and explanation quite intriguing. That made my interest grow bigger and made me thirsty for knowledge.

Along with him, this community includes many more guys who possess a variety of skills. In this community, I was finally able to interact with people who had a higher vision about their lives and they wouldn't settle for a plain, average one.

I started to read as much as I could on human nature, evolutionary biology, social skills, health, business, finance and even game.

When I was learning something, I was implementing it and observed the results. I was trying to get feedback and I was fortunate enough to have people in my social circle capable of offering such feedback to me.

I was going out way more often, interacting with numerous people and refining my methods as much as I could.

As time passes you realize that this is a never ending process. No matter how much of an improvement you think you have done, there is always room for more.

The more you improve yourself the more eager you become to learn and try new stuff. Every time I learn something about a social skill, I want to test it and get feedback. If I see it works, I adopt it and make it part of my belief system. If the results are not what I expected, I try to think what I could have done better or ditch it.

*A tip here is that very rarely you need to ditch something you have read in such a book altogether. Most of the times you need to improve your method of implementation.

Since then, I have read dozens of books, hundreds of articles and I have spent countless hours with like-minded people talking about issues that can help us improve even further.

Unfortunately, I have lost many years doing nothing important. On the other hand, it makes me feel nice that I have found my way even at this stage of my life. Actually most of the people never find it, so I cannot really complain.

Once you take the red pill, there is no turning back.

This is where I am at the moment. This is what I do for a living. I try to become a better man.

(and I also publish eBooks on Amazon Kindle)

But enough about me, let's see what is there for you.

In the following chapters I am going to explain, what I learned from this first year as an Internet entrepreneur.

The struggles I had, the successes, but most importantly the general principles you will need to follow to achieve a level of success at least comparable to mine.

I know this book won't resonate with everyone, but in case it does with you, I am very glad I could help at least one more person achieve financial stability.

Let's go!

Lesson #1

"You will have to be obsessed with your business and 100% committed to it."

This is actually a debate I very often have with my friends and colleagues.

Is it really necessary to love what you do? Do you really have to enjoy doing your business in order to be successful?

Well, to be absolutely honest with you, I am not sure if you need to "love" what you do, but I bet my whole career on what I will state here:

You absolutely have to be obsessed with your business in order to succeed.

Unless you become obsessed with your business, you will not be able to achieve great results. At best, these results will be mediocre and they will take a lot of time to be achieved.

Even if someone ignores what almost every successful man has said about that, I can personally guarantee you this one. Luckily for me I became obsessed with Kindle publishing right away, but I can tell you for sure that all my previous business ventures have failed for this exact reason.

What you read here is not another speech of "love your job", "do what you like for a living", etc. In fact, publishing books is not my favorite thing to do. I prefer to write **articles on my blog for** example.

Publishing books isn't entertainment for me. But I invest many hours thinking about it and working on it. I always think of ways to improve my methods, to implement new marketing techniques, to find new ways to provide valuable content to my readers, etc.

Even when I do something else, and an idea about Kindle pops up in my head, I stop what I do, note it down and then I proceed. But the important thing here is to do it.

Please note this down. Read this previous phrase again. The underline meaning is not that I write down the idea it pops up. **It's the pop up itself**.

When you are obsessed with something, (no matter what this is) your brain works over-hours in order to figure out solutions to optimize this procedure. If you have a serious problem about your business, and you're truly obsessed about it, your brain will try to figure out how to solve this issue on the background.

If it bugs you very badly, you will find a way to solve it sooner or later, even if the idea comes to you while you wash the dishes, or you are out for a walk.

Actually, the best ideas I had up to now, lighted up in my head in a phase I wasn't working on my business. I know it seems a bit odd, but it's 100% sound.

Publishing is not my passion, but it is one hell of a vehicle to get me where I want to go. Financial independence.

I have convinced myself that this is the way I'll do it, and I don't complain about it. I have decided that for the moment this is my way of making money and I'm gonna stick to it.

I am 100% committed, both mentally and physically. My whole life revolves around my business. My daily schedule, my social life, even my phone calls are scheduled around my business.

Business comes first. Everything else is of lesser importance. I have embedded this in my head, so now it doesn't consume my willpower in order to do things that might seem boring.

If it needs to be done, it needs to be done. **There is no boring stuff. There is only stuff that makes money or doesn't.** If I decide that doing all the mundane stuff isn't a good time investment from me, I will outsource it. Not because I am bored, but because my time is invested on a higher end procedure like marketing, keyword research, that will have a better ROI.

Actionable steps

Well, to be completely honest with you, there are no tips to become obsessed with what you do. From my limited experience, I have seen that you either are or not.

Most of the times if it makes money you are going to like it. If it's not profitable you will get tired of trying and you'll drop it.

The catch here is not to give up unless you make absolutely sure that this business won't be profitable in the future. You can only quit after the numbers say so, and not your emotions.

What I have done about it was the following:

When I started with it, I set some "internal" metrics and evaluation points for me. For example:

I said that if this business isn't generating at least $1.000 for me after a year, I will drop it and look for something else.

Of course that was my individual metric, but you get the idea. You can only quit after you have set a realistic goal (based on research and data) and this goal isn't met.

So lesson 1 goes hand in hand with lesson 2.

As soon as you find out something that looks interesting, try to learn about it as much as possible and try to have some successes as soon as you get started.
That way, you maximize your chances to have some early victories that will keep your interest alive. Success after success, your interest will compound to something big.

The more momentum and success you get, the harder will be for you to abandon this. The more successful you become, the more obsessed you will be with that. The more obsessed, the more committed and so on and so forth.

After that, you literally become unstoppable.

Now, this is your business, this is your child. You have seen it grow big and strong. After that, there is no chance you are going to let go. Now you see results. Now you push even harder. **Now you are obsessed and 100% committed!**

Lesson #2

"You have to know your business very well."

After you become obsessed and committed to your business, it will become easy for you to learn your business inside out. If this doesn't happen, you will not be able to compete with everybody else.

You might have heard this many times, but this is really really crucial. Knowing your business very well will make your work way simpler (and profitable).

As a novice publisher I made a ton of mistakes. At first I didn't know how to make a proper keyword research, what a nice e-book cover looks like, how to find good authors who will deliver quality content or even how to promote my books in order to stand out and sell.

And these are only the major parts of this business. Between the lines there is a ton more details to be found and learned.

Same thing applies to every business. Unless you know your business like a real pro, some other pro will "steal" your income.

You might spend hours and hours thinking you do all the right things, but in reality this might not be the case.

You may spend lots of hours trying to figure out why your sales don't go up with no result.

Nobody wants that. Right?

Actionable steps

OK, what's the plan then?

First of all, you will have to study about your business **a lot**. You will need to invest a lot of time and effort in it. But besides that, you will have to work not only hard but smart as well.

Study your competition

Find some successful competitors and try to figure out how they do it. If something works for them, it may very well work for you as well (supposedly you operate in the same niche).

For example, if you want to sell fiction books, try to find out how the big names are doing it and then if possible improve on their methods.

Break down their process step by step. Try to figure out how each component works and what role it plays. Build your own model after this.

Be part of a mastermind group

This one was of tremendous help for me. This is really huge.

Being part of such a team will offer you two very important advantages:

Advantage #1

You will be part of a group with like-minded people. You will hear ideas that are similar to yours, and you will be able to understand and cooperate better with these people.

You will feel part of a team. You will be able to support each other. You are going to push them forward and they will do the same for you.

Every time your own willpower depletes, you will be able to use theirs. There is nothing wrong with that. They should be able to use yours when they feel they need a little push. Fair and square.

Advantage #2

The other advantage is the technical skill you are going to acquire. When you are part of such a group, you will exchange knowledge, techniques and strategies with other people in the same business.

What you might lack in knowledge, might be someone else's strength or vise versa. And the best place to maximize your chances is such a group.

I can't really count the times I asked for a specific answer in my Amazon Kindle mastermind group and they supported me. Actually a big part of my publishing strategy is based on the advice of my fellow publishers.

They have helped me and I have helped them many times over this last year.

We organize online meet-ups with Google hangouts, where we discuss, our latest implementations, results, feedback and next actionable steps.

I can guarantee you, nothing of what I have achieved up to now, would have been possible without their help.

Your capacity as an individual is limited. One of the most important tools you have at your disposal when it comes to master your business is to leverage all the help you can get from other people.

Consume everything there is on your business

When I started on this business, I first watched an online course on how to publish your first book. I liked this course so much that I purchased the second one, then the third etc.

Within months, I had studied lots of books, and articles, and I had watched countless online videos and courses on Kindle publishing.

Some of them were overlapping for sure. But with every new bit of content I learned something new. Sometimes something big, sometimes something relatively trivial.

The important thing here is to be engaged with your business and improve your skill and knowledge in every way possible.

With every new idea you see or hear, you create a new opportunity for your business to take off. With every marketing technique, every copywriting skill, or sales pitch you learn, you approach a step closer to dominating your market and make some serious money out of this.

Lesson #3

"Your family and your friends most likely will not support you."

This actually came as a shock to me. As a wanna-be successful person, you might actually think that your whole close environment will be supportive to your endeavors. Right?

Wrong.

People from your surrounding environment won't be as supportive as you might think, and there are some perfectly fine explanations for that.

Too much social conditioning

No matter what they say to you, bad social conditioning is the main reason people won't be supportive about what you do.

Average people are completely washed out by social conditioning, which implies that having a 9-5 job is the safe way to go. Your friends and your family have been hearing that, for so many years, that this mantra have become a core part of their belief system.

Everything outside their comfort zone makes them feel in danger.

Before I could "prove" to my family that I am capable of living out of my Internet business, I had heard countless times this exact same thing:

> **"Having your own business is**
> **a big risk, go find a normal job**
> **like everybody else"**

Poor guys can't even think for a moment that the risk is where you don't have control. And when you don't you have control I ask?

Exactly, when you don't own the business. Although it has happened to them many times over and over again, they fail to see that. If for any reason (legit or not) your boss wants to fire your ass, he'll do it.

I'll repeat that once more:

Risk = Lack of Control

As long as I have the control of my business (at least up to the maximum possible point), I personally feel safe.

Let your parents and your friends worry as much as they want. I will explain in the actionable steps below that there is not much you can do about it, besides having some actual positive results to display.

Entrepreneurship is out of reality for most people. Unless you are lucky enough to have your father or your mother as an entrepreneur, you will mostly hear negative feedback and a lot of push-back emotional statements.

All you need is constructive criticism. If you cannot get that, screw their opinion all together.

You cannot possibly prove anything of what you do, to them, unless you become exceptional yourself.

It is almost as difficult for you to believe someone who weighs 300 pounds and says to you "I am on a diet." I bet the first thought you will make is that he is joking.

How is it possible for the guy to be on a diet and have that image?

Well in some rare cases it is. He might have started this diet only a few weeks ago. He lost a few pounds but he is still very fat.

The same analogy works for the wealth marathon as well. Only with a big difference. It takes way longer to **have some actual, tangible results** than a diet does.

It might take you a couple of years of hard work, reading, studying, etc. before your business takes off and you have your first successes.

So unless you see that fat guy become lean, you cannot really believe what he's doing really works. Be patient, sooner or later the results will come, and when they come, it's gonna be so sweet!

Most people will be jealous of you

Although your family, won't support you because of their ignorance and lack of vision, many people will be negative about what you do, due to their jealousy.

Most people are by nature **of beta quality.** Mother nature intended this to be like that for her own evolutionary reasons. You can't do much about it either.

You will meet many of those people in your everyday environment. They won't like you to make a progress. Every step you'll make towards your success, the more they will try to bring you down to their level.

Don't fall into this trap. No matter what their agenda is, you don't give a damn about it. You have a greater goal to accomplish. You don't have time to waste on these people.

Course of action

Like I said, there isn't much you can do about overcoming this difficulty but I will briefly mention what I did when I was back in my early stages.

About the jealous ones

This group is actually pretty easy to handle. Whatever you do, you don't get into a serious discussion mode with these people. Their goal is not to help you improve or save your ass from making a mistake.

Their subconscious mind, just pokes them to drug you down with them. No positive outcome will ever come out, when arguing with this kind of people.

Just tell them, what they want to hear and you made it. All they need to hear is that they are right. Don't trust them and don't let them screw your journey to success. You have chosen your path. They have chosen theirs.

There is no harm to hang out with them every now and then, but do know that the more exposure you have to inferior mindsets, the more you skew your reality, and the more difficult your end goal becomes.

About the ignorant ones

This group is actually harder to handle and I will explain why. Most of the times, people in this group will be your family or your close friends. As human beings we tend to have a strong emotional link with our closest peers.

Whenever we hear an opinion from our father, we tend to get it more seriously just because of the fact that he is our father. By nature, we cannot really judge very well whether this is a rational argument or not. Most of the times our father equals authority to us (by default).

Well, I might let you down with this one, but most of the times, in your entrepreneurial life, your family or friends' opinion should be filtered very very strictly.

Just because they love you, doesn't mean they know, what's best for you. Remember what I said earlier? Most probably, they have been victims of the same social conditioning *money is evil*, *you don't need money to be happy* etc.

Do your friends and family care for you?

Absolutely!

Are they successful entrepreneurs?

If yes, then their opinion might be gold, listen to them carefully and try to learn and implement as much as you can.

According to statistics though, most of the times they are simple, average people with no specialized knowledge who just throw opinions **based on ignorance and not facts**.

If your beloved ones, belong to this category all you can do about it is **pace and deflect** while being patient.

This is probably the best technique there is in such a case.

You don't have to explain anything to anyone if they don't want to listen and learn. Just say "I hear you, yes you may be right." That's all they need to hear.

You cannot win this fight by arguing about it. You will only win this fight when your business venture takes off, and you will make a ton of money while they struggle each and every day in their 9 to 5 jobs.

Then all of the sudden, you will become the authority. They will come to you for advice. How do you make money online so easily?

How is it possible to live of the Internet? I wanna do it as well.

From that moment you will know you are on fire. As soon as people start to come to you for business advice, you know you are on the right track.

This by the way is another very profitable business. Teach people how to make money online. While most of online courses "how to make money from home" are scams, yours could be different. By the time you will make money, there is no reason why you can't teach other people how to make money as well – and make some more money along the way ;)

But this is a topic we can discuss on some other book.

For now, all you need to remember is, that you have a greater goal to accomplish in your life. **Your time is way too valuable to be spent on pointless arguments and drama**. Time will prove you (and me) right, and everybody else wrong.

Just tell them to stay tuned.

Your time is gonna come.

And when it comes, it will come with a bang!

Lesson #4

"Stop thinking about you and start thinking on how to serve more people."

This is probably among the most major ones. You hear it very often: "customer always comes first." But what does that really mean?

When I started to build my Kindle business, all I was thinking about was MONEY! I was trying to figure out all the ways I could make more of it. This is not to say I was trying to scam my readers or something, but I have to admit that my first priority was to make a profit and to help these people (my readers) in a meaningful way.

Just to be clear, I am not saying that going after profit is a bad thing. On the contrary. There is no reason to be in any business if you don't make any profit out of it.

But...

This profit will only come after you have served some people with your product or service.

The moment I saw my business take off was when I finally started to "hear" the needs of my customers. I started to ask for continuous feedback on my books. What they liked or disliked. I even gave them some alternatives for the upcoming stories to choose from.

No matter what the nature of your business is, I am sure you can do the same thing with your audience as well.

The major problem is that when you are not 100% transparent and oriented to your customer needs, your potential clients will sense that. Sooner or later they will find out that you are there for the money and not their satisfaction.

And that's just unforgettable in business.

On the other hand, if you make your customer's satisfaction your No. 1 priority, they will see that and they will reward you, with sales which consequently will bring the money.

If you really want to make money, stop thinking "how will I earn 1 million dollars" and start thinking "how can I provide value to people that is worth 1 million dollars".

That is the key point in business. Provide value. Have an impact in people's lives. And you shall be rewarded!

Actionable Steps

OK, now that we are done with all the theory, let's see what we can really do to have a big impact on people's lives.

First and foremost, we will need to make clear some basic points.

Scale and Magnitude

So is it absolutely necessary to impact millions in order to build my wealth empire you will ask

– Short answer is: Yes and No. Let me explain myself by introducing two very simple, yet powerful concepts to you.

Scale

First one is *scale*. I can come up with many ~~not that useful~~ definitions, but I am not going to give you a headache with all these. I will only use a simple one we can all remember (I know how you like simple stuff). By scale we simply mean *"how many units of something we have sold".*

Yep that really is so simple. Whether it is a physical product we talk about, a service, a subscription or whatever you can come up with, scale means in simple terms how many units of that something we can sell. So it makes perfect sense that in order to earn millions we need to sell millions.

By now I think I can hear that little voice inside your brain saying: "big news"...with a grain of irony, but things are not so simple (luckily, because otherwise we would have a hell of a lot millionaires around).

So the million-dollar question here is: "how do I sell millions?"

The not so obvious answer to that, is by creating **value.** The word value is always the cornerstone when you want to sell something to someone. All living animals (humans included) can create value if something is useful to someone else. Therefore, the shortest road to sell millions of something is to have something of value for millions of people, which they will need in order to satisfy one – or more – of their needs.

Let's look at a very classic example here. Let's say we have a very famous football player, one of the best in his generation. Although the "value" he has to offer is not actually tangible – you can't really touch it – it is pretty much there to feel it. He entertains and inspires thousands if not millions of people each day by his performance in the field.

There are many professions like this, driven from people that have the talent or skill to have a big impact on the lives of millions of people. This kind of people like famous athletes, actors, rock stars, even politicians, have made it to the point to be able to impact so many people that society perceives their value to be immense.

Magnitude

Besides scale though, we have one more major factor to count in when we talk about money making. We also need *magnitude.* (That's why I said Yes **and No** in the question before).

Here again I will try to make it as simple as possible for you. By magnitude we mean *"the profit we make out of each sale".* Like scale before, the profit can be on ANYTHING we sell. It does not have to be a car or a toilet (or a car with a toilet). We can make a profit when we sell a service to someone, like being someone's personal coach or counselor or the best salesman in town.

Magnitude is a very important concept as well because it can not only create significant amounts of money, but money that could be achievable with a few sales nonetheless. The most classic example I can think of, is when someone sells for example houses or luxury apartments for instance. He doesn't really need to make a lot of sales (in terms of scale) to earn a lot of money. A few very targeted sales of several million dollars each will suffice.

The Magic Bullet of Wealth

So please cut the crap and tell me how am I going to get rich dude?

I only have two pieces of advice at this point and I am going to analyze them one by one just below. I always try to keep these simple guidelines in my mind for every new business opportunity which may arise before me.

I am not implying that being done otherwise is impossible but, my experience – and more importantly the experience of very successful people in business dictates these two very important principles.

Leave Middle Class Out

That's right. When you try to create a new product or service, always aim for low income class or rich people. Middle class is dead and as time passes it will become even "dead-er". Middle class is a very tricky group to target because of some specific characteristics:

1. **They don't like cheap stuff**, therefore it is very difficult to use this target group to scale.
2. **They don't have enough money to buy expensive stuff**, so the impact or magnitude of each sale won't make a big difference to your business.

If you really want to scale, you really need to look at the low to very low income class. People in this financial bracket will buy all kinds of things as long as they don't cost much like lighters, chocolates, cigarettes etc.

Even better try to give them free stuff by providing the value of entertainment and happiness. Remember the famous football player example? Facebook is another great example of "free" entertaining value giving, that made Mark Zuckerberg one of the youngest billionaires ever.

The second angle to approach this issue, is to aim the wealthy. If you want to leverage your profit per unit or else magnitude, rich people have the spending power to buy exclusive, usually expensive goods.

Their numbers (scale) might not be that big, but their money can be a lot nonetheless. This second road can have its advantages as well. It could take less effort to convince fewer people and it is considered to be of higher status sales policy.

Actually there is not right or wrong as long as you try to aim at these two target groups. If you want to sell a lot (scale), aim for the masses. On the other hand, if you want big profits per unit (magnitude) go for the rich ones.

As an added bonus sometimes middle class will either "drop" their standards and use your "cheap" product, or will struggle financially to buy this new expensive gadget, just to look cool in front of their friends and impress them.

My point here is: Always try to find ways to give "cheap value to the masses or "premium value" to the wealthy ones. Both groups are gonna love it. You can make millions by selling pencils to everybody or a few Ferraris to the have ones.

Remove Yourself

My second requirement – and absolutely necessary this time – is to remove yourself out of the money equation.

Unless you are Tiger Woods or Silvester Stallone – odds are that you aren't – you absolutely need to remove **you** out of the actual money making process. The reason is very simple to imagine, if you have actually read this article, and you have not scrolled down just to drool over this Ferrari.

You Sir are not scalable at all! No matter how many hours a day you work you cannot really scale to impact millions of people, at least not directly. What you really need to do, is to *leverage* your talent in order to impact millions indirectly. You can add tons of value to anyone as long as you use other people's talent **and time**, by working with real stars, but most importantly by solving other people problems.

There is nothing more valuable in this world than some smart, talented individual who can solve another person's problem. Please keep that in mind at all times if you really want to be successful.

Other people needs can be your ticket to financial freedom. No matter how hard I try to think, I cannot come up with a single case of someone who made it for good, without adding massive amounts of value to the lives of millions of people.

As a first actionable step try to come up with an original idea of:

- A new product that will help people to solve a very specific problem
- An existing product that you could improve somehow to become better in a significant way
- A new service to help people save time and effort for some specific task they repeat a lot
- An obsolete service that can be revived to add value again

In this point, I am confident that you have imprinted this very simple but ultra important formula in your heads. When we try to *make millions* we always start by thinking how we can impact as many people as we can in a big way.

We can make a lot of money by having a small impact to millions of people, or having a large impact to a few. Either will work, but we, like perfectionists we are, we always aim for both.

Lesson #5

"Your willpower is limited. Learn how to use it wisely."

This is where the whole game is played actually. The rest of the advice inside this book is mostly technical (how to's). This part is purely a mindset issue. It's a lot more difficult because you will have to tame your beta-quality instincts and emotions to work for you.

Teaching someone how to fish is relatively easy, making him believe that fishing is crucial in the first place, is the really hard part.

I have made this very same conversation countless times with some acquaintances. Proving to them, that taming their willpower is probably the single most important thing they can do, was always of paramount difficulty.

Knowing beforehand that you ain't some average people though, I will take a shot with you!

Your willpower is limited!

That's not really a secret. Moreover, despite the fact that we all understand it subconsciously, we fail to understand how or why that happens.

Imagine you're having a car. In order for the car to accelerate and move it needs to have fuel. The more you step on the pedal, the faster the car goes, but the more gas it consumes.

Willpower is the exact same thing as gas, but for your motivation. As soon as it runs out, you don't feel like doing anything else.

Your willpower tank is usually full in the morning, when you are rested, but during the day it depletes. The harder or longer the task the more willpower it consumes. And this is exactly the reason I am saying it's limited.

At some point, sooner or later you are going to be tired. Not just physically but mentally as well. After your willpower pool is off, you cannot refill it, just like that. You will need to rest through sleep, meditation etc. in order to refill that tank again.

I will try to stretch this out as much as I can, because people don't realize how crucial this is. All of your acts are fueled by your willpower. 99% of the times your action is a matter of your psychological status and not your physical status.

Very seldom your body won't be able to follow your orders. Most of the times it's your mind that "tells" your body to remain idle, because it ran out of willpower.

So in order for you to do **anything**, you will need to make sure that your willpower consumption is optimized so you have enough reserves of it throughout the day.

I know that's easier said than done, but there is hope. I know many people who have optimized this procedure (including myself). It's a quite difficult task to accomplish but not the hardest thing in the world either.

How you are going to achieve that?

1. By avoiding any distraction, which is not aligned to your goal
2. By establishing daily routines

Both difficult and complicated, but both equally important. Let's go on for some technical details on how to optimize this.

Lesson #6

"Establish daily routines to become productive or fail miserably."

Willpower as a resource is finite. That means we cannot increase its capacity forever. I can confirm that by being healthier, living a good life without stress, sleep well etc. can increase the absolute amount of it, but not infinitely.

That is to explain that a guy sitting on a couch all day long, eating pizzas and drinking beers, has by default a smaller tank of willpower than a person, who works, reads, trains and eats healthy.

So after doing all the previous steps and maximize our pools of willpower, now we need to understand how to save as much as possible of this valuable resource in order to be super productive throughout our day.

The first major step in order to harness our willpower is to establish daily routines that will help us expend as low willpower as possible. The more you save, the more you have at your disposal for the more difficult tasks.

I have been through the process of establishing such routines and I can tell you, it wasn't easy!

Once these routines are established though, you will feel so much stronger, energetic and powerful, that you won't go back to your previous state.

Being productive and focused is not an easy thing, especially if you need to do it for prolonged periods of time. Having an end goal, is of tremendous help. If you know *"why"* you need to be more productive, like for example to get a promotion, to grow your business, etc., it will be way easier to have a constant motivation for pushing hard. If your motive is weak, you will eventually get tired and put it aside.

OK, this is the technical stuff, I know you like. What do I need to do?

Step #1: Prioritize max on 3 things

In order to be effective with all the areas you want to increase your productivity you cannot pursue many things at once. Minimize your mid-term goals/projects to 2 or 3. Otherwise you will not have enough energy to accomplish all of them.

It sounds very nice to write for your blog while learning Italian, having two other ventures and learning to play golf, all in the same time. But this is just impossible.

Make a priority list according to your needs and make sure you stick on this. Put all the mid-term areas of improvement in a shorted list and go for it one by one like this:

- Write for my blog
- Automate business venture 1
- Learn Italian
- Learn how to play golf

Step #2: Living on timetable

The absolutely first thing you need to do is to create a detailed timetable and live on this.

I know it sounds very hard right? Well...who said it was gonna be easy. The good thing is that after you make this schedule and you follow it for a few days, your mind will make it a reality (habit) and it will want to follow it on its own. Inside every brain there is a little system called **Reticular Activating System (RAS)**. Among other things, RAS is responsible to make sure that you are safe and sound within every situation. It is most commonly known, for creating your comfort zone.

So for example, you wake up in the morning, you drink your coffee, brush your teeth and then head to work (which by the way, you should have already decided you want to quit and aim for something bigger). This is a habit for your brain and makes you feel comfortable with this pattern. At first, it needs some work to change the *"normal"* pattern of your brain.

So if for some consecutive mornings you wake up, without drinking any coffee and go to the park for running, after a few days, you will feel that this is the normal operation and you will make minimum effort to follow.

Create a very detailed daily schedule, or you can download mine here. Make it fit your life style and all the areas you want to be more productive.

For example, in my schedule, I want to be more productive on my blogging, a venture I have and my reading. Design yours accordingly.

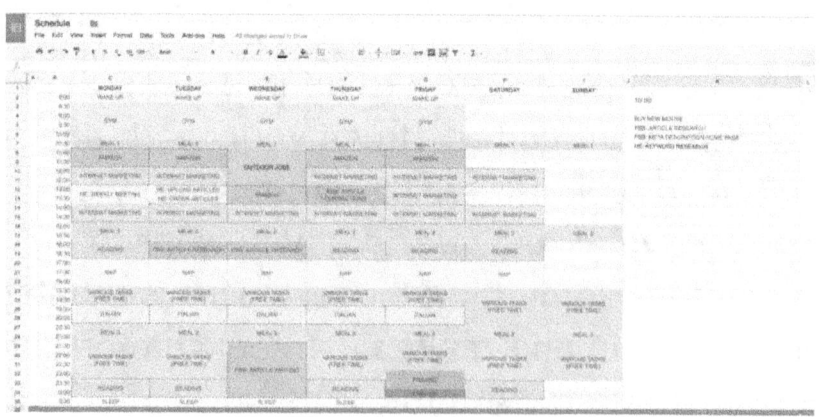

When designing your daily schedule make sure that:

- It is detailed, preferably on a semi-hour basis
- Include **every** task of the day
- Make it as realistic as possible
- Include leisure, rest, sleep, have fun time (you can't work 18 hours a day)

Step #3: Create a to-do list

This is another very important aspect when it comes to organizing. Having in a place, all of the tasks you need to complete, makes it more easy to focus on them. These short term tasks, can be as many as you like, although I would advise you to not let this list grow very big, or else you will lose your motivation on pursuing it.

You can either use:

- Post-it notes
- A sub section within your schedule (this is what I do)
- A white-board on your wall

- An app to remind you all these tasks (all smart-phones have a native app for that)

Step #4: Sleep early and sleep well

Among the biggest hacks, I could offer you today, is this. Simply by improving your sleep cycles you will notice a tremendous difference on your productivity level.

The ideal scenario is to sleep early and wake up early. Depending on some bio-rhythms some individuals are more productive during the morning, while some others during the evening. None though is productive at 3 or 4 o'clock in the morning. Some quick tips to improve your sleep is:

- Try to sleep at least 7 to 8 hours per day
- Sleep during the night (not the other way around)
- Don't over-eat before you go to sleep
- Aim for a dark, quiet environment

Lesson #7

"One day of personal education equals one year of formal education."

In one of my favorite wealth books of all time, "Rich Dad, Poor Dad", Robert Kiyosaki mentions a scene that goes as follows:

Robert was introduced to some rich, successful guy and at some point he asked him: "what is the difference between me and you? How come you are rich and I am not?"

Then the older guy said to him: "The only reason why I am rich while you are not, is that I have the knowledge of how to make money."

This phrase was engraved in my head since then, and if I had to boil it down to a central concept, that might be it.

"The only reason some people are rich, is because they

possess the knowledge of money making."

Sounds simple? Well, it might not be as simple as you think it is. Yet this is the key.

Why is this so important you might ask?

What is there to read and learn that is so important about my success?

Well, I'll tell you what. **Everything!**

Apart from wealth, self-education is of vital importance even when it comes to health or relationship issues.

You cannot possibly expect from your school or your teachers to teach you what you are going to need in your life in order to succeed. If this was the case, our world would be full of millionaires, and poverty would have vanished a long ago.

In this chapter I will narrow down, why formal education will never make you a rich person and why you should always try to educate yourself on your own or with the help of experts in your field.

Most probably there are a lot more reasons, but we are going to analyze those five for the moment, which I consider to be the real *wealth killers*. As usually, for the most loyal and beloved of you, I will also provide solutions, on how to kill the dragon.

Therefore formal education:

1. Kills creativity and original thinking
2. Produces a system of poorly fed rats
3. Promotes competition
4. Flattens dreams and ambitions
5. Lacks training of everyday life skills

Formal education kills creativity and original thinking

In one of the most viewed TED videos ever, Ken Robinson captures the essence of why schools really kill creativity.

Unfortunately, today's educational system only cares about canned answers and ways to think. Teachers, professors and other professionals in the educational field, always choose the easy way to "problem solving". They teach their pupils that, whenever a problem arises, they should look for a pre-made, canned answer to solve it.

As you can understand, this "boxed" way of thinking may be useful for a few, easy tasks, but it can't hold a candle when it comes to hard, real life issues, we all have to face at some point in our life.

Let me illustrate with an example. I bet that most of you have already experienced the situation I am going to describe once or twice in your life. What we learn in schools, is that we all need to get good grades in order to find a *good job* – sigh – to support our family.

What your teacher isn't telling you, is that, your future employer won't give a shit about these (or any other) grades no matter how good they are, as long as you are incompetent to solve a problem on your own and you are constantly seeking for outside help (consuming valuable company's resources).

Try to counter this, by mentioning one situation your good performance in school, helped your promotion in your current job.

In my opinion, the No #1 skill for any employee (not that I advocate to be an employee), is to be able to solve problems in a creative, original way, when they arise. Teach a person to think that way and you may very well skip all the stupid, unnecessary years of formal, linear education, learning mathematics, physics, etc.

Solution

Always try to think outside of the box. Just because there is no canned answer to a problem, doesn't mean you can't come up with an original one (no one has thought before). Don't let anyone, and I mean NONE (even if it is your mother, spouse or your teacher) tell you there are no more original ideas to come up with.

Original ideas DO exist and they are discovered and implemented on a daily basis by talented people, all over around the globe. **Just think of a problem that many people have**, and come up with an original idea to solve it.

Formal education produces a system of poorly fed rats

This might sound bad, but, well...IT IS BAD! Possibly the worst effect of formal education, is that it produces a system of the same copy > paste rats. You have seen them before. Odds are, you are one of them as well. Schools, universities etc. are the best places to breed the super rat species in order to run the economic machine as we know it today.

I can't really think a better way to mass produce, robot employees, than having 30 kids in front of a blackboard, listening to the same blue pill story all day long. Odds for a rat to become excellent (millionaire) are so thin, that I would say, 1 out of 100 rats really stands out to become someone of importance.

The whole thing makes perfect sense, since the well-oiled system does really need, a huge workforce of disciplined rats to run smoothly. To be honest, I am perfectly fine with having rats, but...**I don't want to be one, and neither should you**!

Solution

Get off the hamster wheel now!

How do you expect to thrive if you work on a shitty office for 12 hours a day? You only have that much energy and willpower. Give it a thought!

Nobody forces you to remain a rat on a wheel. I don't fucking care at what age you read this. There is ALWAYS time to make a radical change in your life. Change your job, your friends, your school. Do whatever it takes to stand out from the crowd and live your life by your own means – not somebody else's.

Formal education promotes competition

What a happy thought this is. Since the beginning of our time (as a species), we humans, survived mainly due to our ability to cooperate on multiple levels. Nowadays, economic machine (remember, the one that produces rats), doesn't like that. Today's moto is always about a zero sum game and rarely about real cooperation.

How could it be otherwise, since day one at school, kids learn how to compete for achievements, grades, etc. and rarely learn to cooperate towards a common goal.

Things only get worse at universities (especially the high end ones), where competition is at its finest. Only the best student gets a scholarship, a golden medal or the best looking girl. It is the same story again and again.

If you ask me, I am perfectly fine about the best having the best (this is the whole point of this blog anyway), but I get sick every time I see people ignoring the power of cooperation, in order to promote only their own interests. For better or for worse (depending on which side of the rat wheel you stand), formal educational system very rarely teaches us how to seek for win-win scenarios.

Solution

Win-win scenarios are always what we should look for. When I make a decision, **whether it is for business or for "pleasure"**, I always try to be beneficial for both parties. It will make more profit in the long run even if you can't really see it at an early point.

Competition is only for mindless bullies. Smart decision makers always look to cover their asses and protect the interests of the people they work with.

You have heard for sure the paradigm with the sticks before. One little stick can easily break, two is harder and so on.

Choose your peers (business partners and long term relationships and above) wisely. They can help you, and you can help them back. Together you can achieve new levels of success, that most probably could not achieve on your own.

Formal education flattens dreams and ambitions

Forget about what I said before about the rat making machine. This is the worst of all. Hands down! Of all the curses this alone kills, a huge potential of the innate greatness in all of us. With no exceptions at all, EVERY educational system, whether being school, university or the army, makes you believe that you have no more potential than the guy next to you.

I have yet to meet one single case of someone really believing in me during my younger years – still this may very well be due to being an average guy myself. Granted that I can't really remember a case of someone believing in someone else, as well. I can't really bite it that all the people I have met in all these years, everybody was an average Joe.

There should be some extraordinary ones. Yet nothing. No promotion, on a mental or practical level. We all learn to be the same. No educational system (that I am aware of) will make you believe and pursue your dreams and ambitions. Instead they will make an excellent job feeding you the blue pill of "averageness" during your most sensitive years.

Solution

Don't be a victim as well. You don't have to kill any of your dreams. Anything is possible, as long as you believe in it. Who is your teacher to tell you that you can't make millions. Most probably a really under-paid rat, that can't see further than his nose.

If your goal is to be a millionaire or to fuck models, it is entirely in your hand to achieve this. Just break the process into smaller pieces/sub-goals and try to make one step at a time. Eventually you'll get there!

Formal education lacks training of everyday life skills

Another biggie. I wasn't really curious about it during my child years. But eventually it hit me in the head. What the hell do I really need history, astrology, poetry, arts, etc.? Courses like these don't add a single bit of value to my life. Period!

I am not saying that we don't need any of those, but studying about a stupid war that took place a gazillion years ago by someone to conquer something (mind you: which most probably is a propaganda book, written by our own government) won't help me a tiny bit to achieve my goals, any time sooner.

Real life skills and problem solving are crucial weapons in order to survive and thrive.

General knowledge about poetry, arts and history is – good to have knowledge – as long as you have a tone of spare time and you want to cultivate your cultural background.

Solution

I have to admit, this is a hard one. Since school will fill your kid's head with a shit load of useless information. I have really thought about it in the past. Only feasible solution I have found is to let my kid go to school for a few years in order to learn the basics. That would be some basic mathematics, the native language, plus a couple more languages, and that's it.

Rest of self-education should be about:

- evolutionary biology
- anthropology
- applied psychology
- social skills
- money making
- networking
- critical thinking
- problem solving

But most of all, **education about your business!**

That's it. As long as my child learns about these things, I believe he/she would be able to cope with most of the situations life will throw at his/her face and **thrive**!

Competitive advantage

If I have not convinced you by now, I got one more arrow in my quiver. Simply think of this.

Who else does what I just described? **Very few people**. Usually the most exceptional ones (what a coincidence).

What I just described is what 90% of people out there won't do. They are just mimics who simply copy what others do (very unsuccessfully). Your main strength, your powerful weapon, your personal angle will be exactly that.

Your specialized knowledge. The more you know your industry the better results you are going to have. The more you know your business the more frequently and of better quality will be the ideas that will pop up in your head.

I have seen it countless times on my businesses up to now. The more I educate myself about it, the more I read, the more I discuss, the better I become.

All of a sudden the better you become at something, the better your mind works in that area. It's kind of "magic" but it's true. Mother nature gave us this weapon in the past and now we can use it in our favor by consciously stir our mind towards the route we want.

Lesson #8

"No matter what you do, avoid distractions at all costs."

Although I don't have any unimportant issues in this book (why would I anyway), this is actually pretty big.

Distractions in our daily lives kill our productivity and therefore our success. The worst part is that these killers are so stealth, that you cannot really spot them and eliminate them.

Moreover, just to make things a bit worse, these distractions, step on our innate laziness as human beings, making the whole process of eliminating them a real tough job.

But like every difficulty I have mentioned up until now, eliminating distractions from your life is a totally doable procedure by the moment you make up your mind about it.

After I have started to use the tools which I will mention in a moment, in order to track my productivity score, I realized that a huge chunk of my daily time was spent in vain, due to these stupid distractions.

I spent more than 30 minutes a day in Facebook alone. I mean come on. That's 15 hours a month!

I thought at that point that if I wanted to have any major success I should do something about it. I thought that if I spend these 15 hours a month in my Kindle Publishing business, I will see a huge spike in revenue.

And I was dead right. By the time I cut the crap, avoid every possible distraction and gave full focus on my business, it really took off.

If you follow the steps mentioned in lesson 5, lesson 6, and lesson 8, you will very soon see your productivity levels skyrocket.

If you don't believe me, give it a go for only a month. If you don't see any noticeable difference, then throw this book in the recycle bin and log in back in Facebook.

So how am I going to avoid all distractions?

Boom! If you thought the first part of lesson 6 was difficult, let's see what you can do here. Assuming you have already made a detailed schedule, distractions throughout the day alone, could kill your productivity like that. Following the steps below, will help you eliminate 80% of those distractions and step up your game.

Step #1: Forget about multitasking

Here comes the first shock. Contrary again to the general belief, we humans, are not good at multitasking. That is performing two or more tasks in the same time. Driving and talking to the phone, having sex and reading a magazine etc.

While it is possible to be done (at least the second one), it is far from optimal. The reason behind this, is that your brain in order to perform an action takes a series of steps:

1. Gathers visual and other sensory information
2. Compares the live actual situation with the desired one
3. Calculates all the necessary actions in order to achieve the desired result
4. Commands all the parts necessary to help towards this direction

Every time you want to switch to a new task you force your brain to recalculate a whole lot of variables. While this might seem easy and trivial, it really is not. If you make your brain to make such calculations again and again you always operate at a sub-optimal level and you will get tired fast.

Imagine being in front of your pc and writing on something. Due to limited brain capacity (unfortunately each of us is given one brain) your brain makes some initial calculations/estimations when you sit on your desk. You subconsciously enter a writing state where,

- your brain allocates a lot of resources on the creative part of this writing (the part that needs to do the actual thinking)
- it takes for granted (no energy consumed) things on your surrounding environment (keyboard, computer screen etc.)

While you stay at this task your brain doesn't have to make all the basic calculations again (where you are, what you look at, what you hold) so you may proceed at full brain capacity on this task alone.

Even the slightest of distraction, like your phone, the doorbell, your spouse yelling at you, will make your brain make a whole lot of new calculations again, by allocating the corresponding resources (there is no other way really).

So whatever you do try to stay focused at one thing at a time. That is why the timetable is of extreme importance. Each task has its allocated time slots during the day and you make sure you stay as close to this as possible.

Step #2: Throw the TV out of the window

Not much to say here really. TV is the perfect productivity (and success) destroyer. Unless you own the TV channel, there is absolutely no fucking reason to even have a TV in your house.

99% of TV's content is pure trash. For the 1% remaining, I bet you can find the same content on Internet as well. TV's bad aspect is two-fold though. You not only lose precious time with a huge opportunity cost but you also get washed with bad social conditioning. You get *shampoo and conditioner* in one product.

Try to minimize your TV time exposure as much as possible. If you cannot throw it out altogether, at least spend the least amount of time possible.

Step #3: Log out from social media

This is a no-brainer either. Social media are responsible for a huge chunk of wasted time throughout our day. Chatting with your friends on Facebook or watching funny kitten videos on Youtube ain't productive at all.

There is a million other ways you can use social media to your advantage and we will talk in detail about these in the future. But for now, log out from any social media distraction, at least for the time you need to be productive. You may very well schedule a particular chunk of your day dedicated on your social media frenzy. As long as it is predefined and within normal limits (max 1 hour / day – if you absolutely must do it), then you stay in the safe zone.

Useful Tool #1: A very nice tool I use in order to monitor my productivity on the web is called RescueTime. This tool will let you see in a glance how productive you are throughout the day. By assigning roles (distracting, productive etc) to each website, RescueTime will tell you what percentage of your time is spent to which website.

It has also the functionality to lock specific domains from your browser for a specified amount of time (remember the kittens on Youtube)?

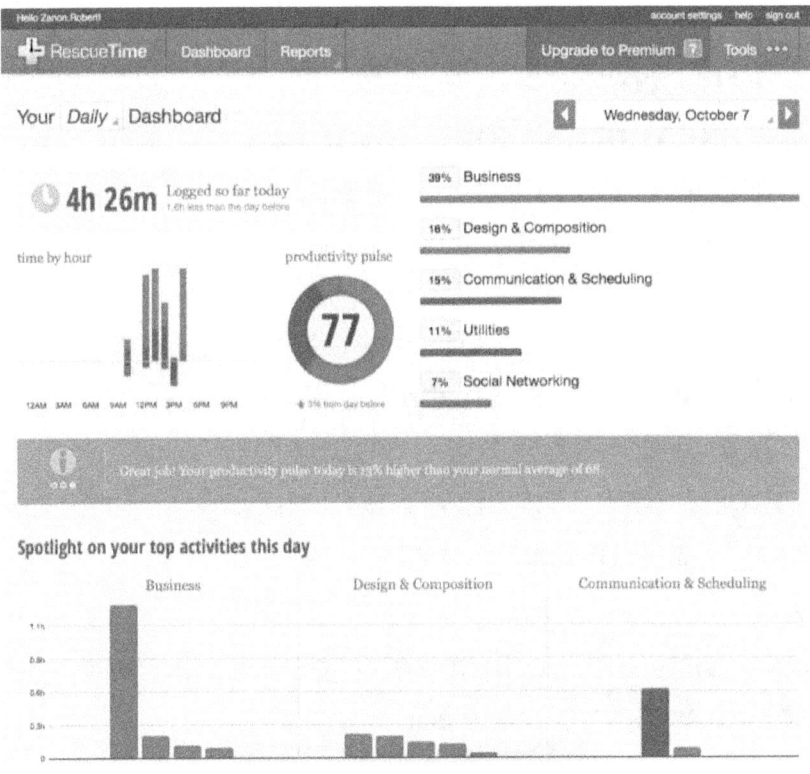

Step #4: Pomodoro technique

Pomodoro technique is among the best I have found around productivity optimization. It is a very basic concept based on the famous pomodoro timer, used by chefs and housemaids in the kitchen.

Pomodoro technique works as follows:

1. Start by focusing on a single task for **25 minutes**
2. Take a break for **5 minutes**
3. Repeat this cycle 4 times
4. Take a longer 15-minute break

It is scientifically proven that human brain likes to work in such cycles. Depending on each individual or task, you might need to change this interval, for example 45 minutes focus – 15 minutes break.

Start with the default settings and adjust according to your needs.

Under no circumstances, should you break those 25 minutes. No distractions at all. Turn every notification, phone or doorbell off and stay 100% focused on your task. Even a tiny distraction will cause your brain to lose focus. Focus that will cost you energy to get back. In case some flash thought crosses your mind (something you need to do for example) switch to your notebook, note it down and get back to your main task. Don't waste more than 5 seconds on that.

Always take your break. Never skip on your break. It is important to take it in order for the brain to take a rest. During those 5 minutes you can get up your chair, take a short walk, go to the bathroom, have a little water etc. Do whatever you want to do as long as it is relaxing. Even a relaxing song might help you here.

Useful Tool #2: There are many apps designed to help you stay on track with pomodoro. I would suggest you to try them out for two reasons. First of all, you will get **an extra motivation**, that someone is "watching you" and therefore make you feel more accountable. Secondly, you will be able to track down all your productivity hours during the day/week/month. Moreover depending on the app you will use, it is possible to separate these pomodoros to every task/goal you want to achieve (4 pomodoros on blogging, 6 pomodoros on Italian learning etc). Here is the application I personally use, called **Pomodoro Time**.

My First Year as an Internet Entrepreneur

vious week	This month	Previous mo

Start date	1 January 2016
End date	12 January 2016
Task	All tasks

Pomodoros	118
Completed tasks	0
Duration	49:10:00

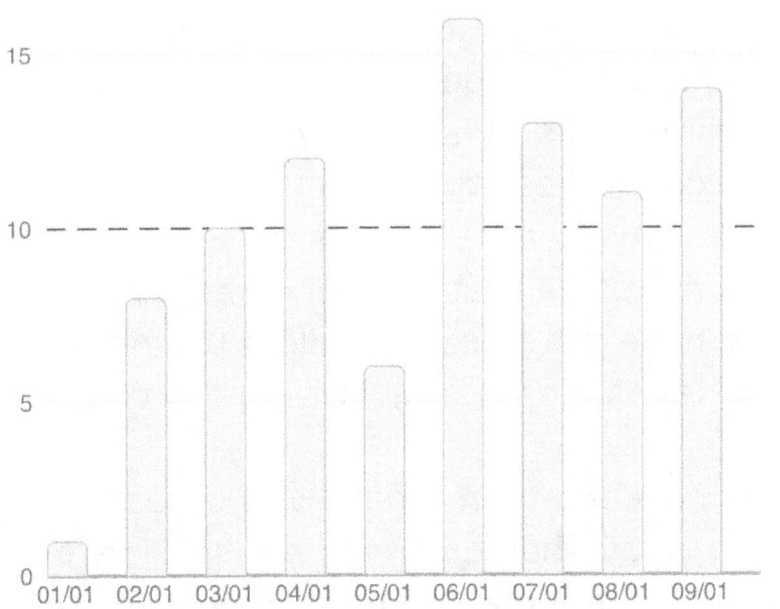

Useful Tool #3: Something that really helps me to focus here is to have a mild background noise of around 60db's. Don't ask me again...Scientifically proven as well. Sounds around 60db's will help your mind relax quite a bit and will promote your focus ability. Here is an excellent iPhone and Mac application called Noizio that mimics some nature sounds, like the sea, fire, wind, etc.

Step #5: Reward your self

Final point but a very important one. You have made a lot of effort to stay on track, you logged out of Facebook, you didn't answer your girlfriend's calls, you even broke your TV. Although all these things will boost your productivity by a lot, results on your success might not come that fast. Imagine that you might have set a goal to build a business that might takes month or even years to complete.

Every now and then (again with proactive design), you should reward yourself for the hard effort you make. That way your brain's reward center will associate this whole effort with something positive, giving you an extra motivation to push forward.

For example, once a week you can party with your friends, once a month take a short trip for a weekend or even schedule that every 100 pomodoros you will make a small present to yourself. Whatever works for you really. The important thing here is again to be proactive and have the whole thing planned from the beginning.

Buying yourself a 5k $ watch because you passed outside a jewelry shop ain't rational at all. But if you make a note to buy yourself this watch only when you accomplish a very important task (ie. earn your first 100k $ from your business)...There, this is a very nice, well thought and well deserved reward for you.

Lesson #9

"To reach success you have to fix your environment first."

I left this lesson as a last one, because it's probably one of the most important and difficult ones to accomplish. What I am going to write in this chapter might sound harsh to you, but believe me, it's all 100% true.

When you will be reading this chapter, you might wonder what the heck has your environment has to do with your future success? And how my environment played a vital role in my first steps as an entrepreneur?

Please do move on. I am pretty sure you'll get it.

No matter how cynical you may think these words are, they reflect reality like nothing else.

"We don't have a money tree"

An old time classic.

Among my favorite phrases of all time.

Although I cannot complain about what my mother offered me as a child, I sure have heard this phrase a lot of times.

"We don't have a money tree."

A golden goose, a money printing machine, and all this *special equipment* someone needs to make some serious money.

The main inspiration about putting together this chapter, was a startup company summit that was once held in my city.

Apart from all the technical stuff (which are not that important) I have also seen a whole different world of successful people with well-worked mindsets.

The true catch, though, was not the summit or the mindsets, but a single phrase one of the keynote speakers (Nikos Bonatsos) said at the end of his speech. The guy is Greek, but he left Greece a few years ago in order to work as a venture capitalist for General Catalyst.

What he said was:

> *"It makes perfect sense not to see many successful entrepreneurs. How would it be possible for anyone to become successful when he hasn't seen how success looks like."*

Bang!

It really hit me in the head. It was one of these a-h-a moments you have in your life and they alter your reality, possibly forever.

It made perfect sense to me as well. If you grow up among average people, you subconsciously set your success limit according to their level.

Nobody wants to destroy you on purpose, your mother and father love you very much (I assume), your friends want your best interest as well.

Then what the hell is going wrong?

It's very simple. They are people with average mindsets, average skillsets but most of all, average ambitions. Like you did, most of them have already grown up in such a similar, ***uninspiring*** environment as well.

If averageness is all you live, averageness is all you seek.

My mother didn't have a money tree (I know for sure now), because she grew up, believing it's impossible to plant such a tree. Her father and mother, her schoolmates and her whole environment had never seen such a tree.

To be honest, I didn't believe it was possible to plant such a tree a couple years ago. It's pretty damn hard (or should I say -

impossible) not only to imagine of something that you have never seen but also to believe in it as well.

The law of averageness

I am not just talking about **social conditioning** here. I am talking about a 100% broken reality. By the time someone of us is born, all he sees is averageness. People with no ambitions, living paycheck to paycheck and waiting to die quietly a few years later.

People who aren't going to be missed by anyone if they're run over by a bus - OK maybe I've gone too far, they will be missed by a few (mostly relatives).

I don't know about you, but I had (I still do sometimes) a very hard time, leaving this kind of environment behind me. I have given up with most of my friends, I often disagree with my mother on many issues, I even have a hard time having a conversation with most of my girlfriends.

People just don't get it. Most probably they will never do. **Success and greatness are 100% out of their reality**. In fact, it's so far out of their reality, that every time I mention words like success, money and abundance they look at me like I am some crazy scientist talking about space trips to Mars.

The worst part is that none of us can consciously understand what is going on here. Having a cheap-ass neighbor, or friends and family with a scarcity mentality, poisons your mind with averageness.
You are taught to be poor, average and unsuccessful, not because your family or friends want you to be, but simply because they are themselves.

As a kid, you have all the mechanics in place to help you stay alive in the jungle. Remember this is how you are programmed by nature. On the other hand, these mechanisms might become evolutionary traps if you don't learn how to overcome the default mode. Two of these mechanisms are:

Mechanism #1: Mimicry

As a child, when you were born into the jungle you had some automatic mechanisms in place, that could improve your chances for **survival and reproduction**. Mimicking what other people are doing is such a mechanism.

If you really think about it, that makes perfect sense. If you see someone else doing something and surviving, your brain subconsciously draws the conclusion that this is OK to mimic. Energy preservation (laziness) will take care of the rest, making sure you won't try to **think and act differently**. Actually, this is one of the most powerful weapons, we as humans have. We have a pretty amazing skill in copying other people's behavior, mannerisms, acts, etc.

Most of the times we don't even have to discuss about it. *Monkey sees, monkey does.* If you see you father struggling through his whole life, you pretty much assume this is the way that it's supposed to be. If you see all your friends growing up becoming average people, this is the level you are going to set for yourself as well.

If your father told you, that money isn't easy to make, who are you to say the opposite? You take his words for granted, and you can only dream about this Ferrari, you once saw passing by.

Mechanism #2: Be part of the team

The second mechanism that has serious implications is very difficult to overcome as well. Again, based on evolutionary reasons, we want to be liked by other people very much. Nowadays having a few people that don't like you might be OK, back then though, this was a very serious issue.

Nobody wants to be disliked by his social circle. And we try to protect ourselves from becoming unprepossessing all the time. We want other people to like us, so we try to "blend in" in every environment we are.

Although on average it is a good tactic not to break the rapport with average people, it can be very dangerous. Average people tend to be lazy, unproductive, with scarcity mentality and a boatload of other **beta characteristics** on them. Whether you like it or not, in order to blend in, you will have to adopt some of them in order to become part of the team.

Example: One of the most typical examples (especially here in Greece) is when you find yourself among a company and they start to talk about the economic crisis. You hear phrases like, *"we get screwed by the government"*, *"we can't stand this anymore"*, *"life is unbearable",* etc. And all I can do is a nod and say, *"Yeah, you are absolutely right. I can't stand these fuckers."*

Now, you see the obvious problem here?

The problem is that I don't really give a fuck about the government or the crisis. A man who is destined to succeed will succeed anyway, but I have to "agree" on a superficial level in order to maintain rapport with these average people. Although I know consciously that I don't give a tiny rat's ass about the government or the crisis, hearing these useless messages all day long ruins my reality a big time.

May the force be with you

So here they are two opposing forces. Two voices I have inside my head.

On one side I have all the role models I admire. All these great guys who are achievers and have done some great things with their lives. Most of the times, what they preach is right and they possess an extraordinary mindset.

On the other side, I am surrounded by average people, who like me, have swallowed the blue pill of mediocrity and most of the times, their beliefs make me wanna puke.

I always try to remember that maintaining rapport with them is a very basic social skill, every successful man has to possess. So I'm gonna tell you the exact same thing here. Average people are absolutely necessary and you have to learn to co-exist with them - *but not for prolonged periods*.

The more you hang out with the *wrong* mindset type of people, the more your belief system will be poisoned with averageness.

Unfortunately, (for you) there is not much to be done while you are a kid. Most of your decisions will be taken by your folks, who most likely are only normal people.

By the time you become a teenager, then it's the time to put your foot down and make up your mind. You either live and die an average guy, or you bust your balls, you give your 100%, and **you live and die an achiever**.

You don't have to settle for mediocrity. You haven't signed a contract you know? You just made a very strong and very bad (admittedly) subconscious deal with your family and society when you were born.

So what? Screw that deal. You were only a kid, you didn't know what you signed for anyways.

Stand up and say to yourself, I am not going to die an average guy. I want to make an impact in this world. I don't want to be another invisible ant, someone stepped on because I wasn't big enough for him to see me.

I want to matter!

I know what I am saying is actually hard to implement. How is someone supposed to know if he is affected by the law of averageness or not?

Well, the quick answer is that you are.

No doubt about it, I bet my money on that. But in case you have doubts and you wanna bet as well, please take some time and **read these 5 books:**

1. Rich Dad Poor Dad – Robert. T. Kiyosaki

2. The Millionaire Next Door – Thomas J. Stanley
3. Secrets of the Millionaire Mind - T. Harv Eker
4. How Rich People Think - Steve Siebold
5. The Millionaire Fastlane - MJ DeMarco

If what's written in these books is aligned to your reality then you either: (A) should be very successful, or (B) you know what success is and you fight day by day to get there.

In case your reality includes paradigms of (A) formal education, (B) linear thinking and (C) reactiveness, then you have a hard bumpy road ahead.

Conclusion

Fortunately (for me and a few other people), I was *lucky* enough to meet some people that helped me take the red pill, and face the truth as it is. Once you take the pill, there is no turning back.

Most of the words in this book are supposed to achieve exactly that. Feed you the red pill of knowledge in order to wake up and overcome the law of averageness. In order to believe that there is a bigger picture. In order to believe that you don't have to live and die an average person.

In order to believe that you can plant a money tree yourself.

This was just the beginning

I hope you really liked this book but most of all, I hope it will help you in your first steps as an Internet Entrepreneur.

I hope I didn't get you tired with all my stuff. I tried to keep it as simple and short as possible. But in the same time, I didn't want to leave anything valuable outside.

These were the most important lessons I learned as an entrepreneur during my first year.

I made a lot of mistakes, I lost a few battles, but I keep pushing. I am not going to give up, until I reach my financial freedom, and then we'll see how it goes.

It's a long road, but I am more than willing to walk it.

I hope I will have you with me on this long journey.

If you want to contact me, you will find me in my personal blog: projectbebest.com

Thanks a lot.

Kind regards
Roberto Zanon

www.ingramcontent.com/pod-product-compliance
Lightning Source LLC
Chambersburg PA
CBHW070324190526
45169CB00005B/1729